*The Truth about Sex by High School Senior Girls*

Book design by Dunn & Associates, Wisconsin

Publisher's Cataloging in Publication
Anderson, Kristen.
The Truth about Sex by High School Senior Girls/
Kristen Anderson
        p.        cm.
Summary: Provides data from survey of high school seniors about sex, encourages abstinence as an alternative to regretful consequences
    ISBN  0-9708831-0-2
1. Sexual ethics for teenagers 2. Sexual abstinence 3. Sex-miscellanea. I. Title.

LC Catalog Card Number 2001116805


First Printing:  May 2001

Printed in the United States of America

# The Truth about Sex by High School Senior Girls

# Contents

*You shall know the truth, and the truth shall make you free.*
*John 8:32*

## Chapter 1

## *The Truth about Sex*

Ashley, 16, worked in a video rental store after school. She wasn't interested in any of the guys in her class, and the guys she would be interested in all had girlfriends, anyway. Gary, 21, another employee at the video store, seemed to be flirting with her lately. One night they were both closing together, and Gary suggested they go back to his house.

Crystal, 14, hooked up with Josh, a cute guy she met at summer camp. One night they arranged to meet after everyone had gone to bed. They were making out and Josh started to take off her pants. Crystal knew she didn't want to have sex, but she offered to "go down on" Josh instead. The next day, Crystal felt really embarrassed about the whole thing, and wished she could go back in time and change things.

Amber's friends all had boyfriends, and she was getting tired of being left out of all their conversations about relationships and sex. She started to feel like an outcast, and like she was losing her best friend, Heather. She considered "doing it" with a guy she knew was interested in her so she could maintain her closeness with her friend Heather, and so she would feel like she fit in with her group of friends.

Laura and Kim wrote notes to each other since they didn't have any classes together this year. Laura asked Kim how many times she and Tyler had done it. Kim wrote back that it had been 15 times, including in the shower last week in Tyler's house. Laura wrote that they should have a contest to see who could do it the most in the next two weeks.

Melissa's parents divorced when she was seven. Melissa's mom had to work late shifts at her job, and her dad had recently remarried and moved to another state. Melissa had the house to herself a lot, and she started to have guys over to have sex when her mom was at work.

Alicia and Chase had been going out for almost a year. Alicia really liked Chase, and she wanted to keep going out with him, but she wasn't sure she was ready to have sex. Things were getting tense between them, the subject kept coming up, and then he started hinting around about "finding someone who will."

Jennifer woke up Sunday morning with a hangover and very little memory of the night before. She stayed in bed most of the afternoon, and told her parents she might have a touch of the flu. She called her friend Nicole to see if she could help her figure out what exactly had happened the night before. Jennifer was pretty sure she had slept with Joe, but she was a little fuzzy on who had initiated it, and where he went later. She didn't think he was in the car when Nicole drove her home.

Sarah and Chris, both 19, attended a Christian college. Despite their religious beliefs, Chris and Sarah started to sleep together. In December of her sophomore year of college, Sarah found out she was pregnant. Sarah tearfully broke the news to her parents over Christmas break. Chris's parents forbade him to see her, and they denied that the baby was his.

Jessica was having trouble concentrating in school. Only a few weeks ago, she had been dating Justin. They went out a few times, and ended up having sex at Justin's house when his dad wasn't home. Jessica was sure their relationship was going to get serious, but Justin hadn't called in several days. Then Jessica heard that Justin had been seen hanging around a freshman girl lately.

Christina had a reputation for being a party girl. She had had sex with twelve guys by the time she was seventeen. Most of the time, she never intended to have sex with them, but she would get drunk at parties every weekend, and then would get too carried away with a guy at the party. It was always fun at the time, but she rarely heard from the guys after that, sometimes they even ignored her at school the following week.

Amanda ran into Tonya in the girl's bathroom at school. They started talking about a party where Tonya said DeShaun would be. Tonya was friends with DeShaun's ex-girlfriend, but she still encouraged Amanda to go after him. The girls giggled and high-fived, and Amanda strutted out of the bathroom saying she was going to "get DeShaun" that night.

Tiffany, 14, had had her eye on Eric for a long time. He was a senior, he was rich, cute, and popular, and he had finally started paying attention to her! One night Tiffany met up with Eric at a party, and they left in Eric's car. They started making out, Eric put his hand up Tiffany's skirt, and then he put Tiffany's hand on his crotch. Tiffany was a virgin, but she didn't want to mess up any chances she had with Eric, so she let him have sex with her.

If any of these situations are familiar to you, or if you are confused about when and with whom you will have sex, this book is written for you. Like any teenage girl, you receive different messages about sex from many different sources. If you're lucky, someone sometime has told you that sex is designed to be a sacred emotional, physical, and spiritual bond between a man and a woman who love each other and who are committed to each other. That's the <u>truth</u> about sex. But it's easy to get confused in today's society by all the other things you see, hear, and read about sex. Sometimes people that we look up to don't even seem to have it right. (Former President Bill Clinton is the classic example here).

There are so many different portrayals and messages about sex in our culture, but it's surprising how infrequently any of the messages you hear or see are actually THE TRUTH. On TV, every time a man and woman have their first kiss, the very next scene predictably and inevitably shows them in bed. Believe me, it is not always such a straight shot from first kiss to sex! The next time you're watching TV, you can count five seconds after the new couple starts their first kiss. Then the camera will cut to the bedroom, the next morning, after they've slept together. Really! It's so predictable!

One senior girl writes, *"I think that in magazines and on TV there is a lot of emphasis on teens having sex. For example, on 'That 70's Show,' Donna was kind of treated like an outcast for not doing it with Eric sooner."*

On the radio and on MTV, there are lots of songs and videos about sex. Of course the sexual element of popular music makes it fun and exciting. No one wants to be a prude about songs like, "It Wasn't Me": "Picture this-we were both buck naked banging on the bathroom floor." Lots of rap videos show barely dressed women prancing around for the rapper to do with as he pleases. But at the same time, if all the songs and videos about casual sex cause you to believe that life is one big orgy, you have not heard the truth.

In the popular 1999 movie, "American Pie," Tara Reid's character is debating whether to have sex with her boyfriend. She consults her worldly "friend" who balks at the fact that Reid's character has never even had an orgasm. First of all, it is highly unrealistic for a 17 year old girl to attain orgasm, second of all, that is not good advice.

And what ever happened to Baby and Johnny in the 80s classic, "Dirty Dancing" after Baby went away to college? That was quite a summer romance, but in real life they both would have to go their separate ways in the end.

Last time I checked, the printed media for teenage girls was more straightforward. Mostly they say, "Only you will know when the time is right for you to have sex." What they don't tell you is that what can seem like the right time usually turns out not to be.

If you feel you have graduated from "Seventeen" and "YM" into magazines like "Cosmopolitan" or "Mademoiselle," you'll definitely get an eyeful of misleading articles about sex. I don't think articles like, "Men Tell: What Makes a Woman a Good Lover," and "60 Sins You and He Should Commit" are truly helpful to girls. Or grown women, for that matter. #5 on the list of sins was, unbelievably, "Why not sleep with more than one guy in 24 hours if you really like them both?" #41 was, "Buy a mega condom dispenser and keep it stashed in your bedside table. When you have an overnight guest, open the drawer and just unfurl." Gross.

The magazines make it seem like that's "just the way it is." Articles about wild one-night stands, and about living together as the status quo in relationships make it seem like you will live that way too when you get older.

The internet explosion has been an incredible advance in the information market, bringing us facts and opportunities we wouldn't otherwise have known about. The downside to the internet is the garbage that it also makes so available to us. It's quite easy for children to stumble upon or look for sexually inappropriate images. There are hundreds of sites that advertise "hot young sluts" or webcams of pornographic acts. And the internet has also allowed another avenue for sexual predators to reach innocent children through chat rooms and email that may be unsupervised by caring adults.

Even if you don't take to heart any messages from TV, movies, magazines, etc., it may still seem that, indeed, everyone IS "doing it." I did a survey of my former students where the survey forms were anonymous, and the results showed that only 50% of senior girls surveyed have had sex. That hardly constitutes EVERYONE. Of the 50% who have had sex, 74% regretted sexual experiences they had! That's a lot of girls regretting what is supposedly a great time. Why do you think young women are feeling this way about having sex?

Other messages that girls get about sex come from the guys. They may imply that they wouldn't be interested in a girl unless she would have sex. So a girl thinks that sex is the thing she can use to get and keep a guy's attention. Or she may think that sex is the way to be a good girlfriend, to give him everything he wants; to live for HIS happiness, in other words.

A lot of the messages girls get about sex come from their friends. 65% of senior girls surveyed said that, *"Most of my friends have had sex."* When your friends have had sex, it makes it seem like sex is the right thing for you, too. Your girlfriends may not tell you if they have regrets about sex because sometimes it hurts to admit a painful mistake.

Parents and adults can give mixed messages about sex. They can be confused about it, too. Sometimes nobody has told them the truth about sex, either! Some parents make it seem like sex is bad and wrong. Some parents are on the other end of the spectrum, though. They might be divorced and sleeping with or living with a new boyfriend or girlfriend. In that case, the message about sex can be that sex is just something you do with whoever you happen to be with at the time.

Finally, a girl's beliefs about sex may come from her own mind. Maybe you have told yourself that a guy won't like you unless you sleep with him. Maybe you have told yourself that sleeping around is part of being popular. Maybe you consider it a gift to a guy, to show him how much you like him, or to show him that you are a fun-loving girl. Maybe you have told yourself that you're not responsible for the things that happen when you're drunk. Or you have told yourself that if a guy wants to have sex with you, it's because he likes you, and he thinks that you're attractive. Have you convinced yourself that having sex will make you feel less lonely, or that it means you are loved? Do you believe that sex is "just something people do," and will you walk blindly into a situation you will ultimately regret?

One senior writes, *"I think my sister has sex to feel loved. I see her doing it too often, and I see how much it hurts her. Sex is important and should be with someone who you know already cares."*

This book is not anti-sex. My purpose is not to tell you that sex is bad, or that people who have sex are bad. Sex can be an amazing, glorious experience, BUT ONLY WITH THE RIGHT PERSON, IN THE CONTEXT OF A COMMITTED RELATIONSHIP. Outside of a committed relationship, sex brings disappointment and heartache, and it can leave deep emotional scars. Think about it: when you give someone a part of yourself, that is a momentous act. If that person is not committed to you, they have no concrete plans to be around in the future. So you have given yourself to someone who can eventually leave, and that can really hurt.

What is a committed relationship? A marriage is the most sacred and beautiful commitment between two people. But what about high school relationships, two people who have been going out for several months, couples who are "serious"? Aren't those committed relationships?

In high school, although two people may be exclusive, and they may love each other, there usually is not a commitment beyond graduation. So there really aren't any guarantees, although there may be a very strong bond between a couple. Couples can break up, one may move away, or go away to college, or find someone else, or just decide they would rather spend time with their friends than be in a relationship. There are lots of changes and things that happen in high school. How many high school sweethearts do you know that are married today? In other words, the chances of a high school relationship surviving into adulthood and marriage are very slim. So, although a high school relationship may be very loving, it generally doesn't count as a *committed* relationship.

If you are in a serious relationship, I don't want to make light of your relationship. I just want to emphasize the fact that marriage is the only <u>true</u> guarantee of a commitment. Things in high school are unpredictable, and sex is definitely a decision you should be sure of and feel safe about. It is not a decision to make in unpredictable circumstances. Two people can say they are committed to each other, but they might mean they are committed UNTIL... Until they break up, go to college, until feelings change, etc. That's not a commitment because one of them can break it off whenever they decide it's time.

Marriage is a promise to be a partner, lover, and friend for life. Dating, relationships, and even living together do not involve the commitment that only marriage signifies. Marriage means that two people vow to stay together, work together, for better or for worse, to be exclusively with one another for the rest of their lives.

Yes, that is what is supposed to happen, despite the heartbreaking divorce rate in our country. But many girls see marriage as a gamble. One girl writes, *"I don't know if marriage is the only sure thing because in my family that is not what I see, or in society in general. It <u>should</u> be that way, but nowadays it really isn't in the majority."*

The good news is that you do have control over whether or not you will have to go through a divorce. You can choose someone who also feels that marriage is forever. You can marry a man who will not give up after some arguments, a man who would be sick at the idea of having an affair. You can marry a man who wants to and will go the distance with you, a man who won't quit after 3 years, 10 years, 20 years!

What if there was a ceremony in this country that revered and respected a young woman's first time? A gathering of all the young woman's family and friends, a celebration of the sexual bond that will form between the girl and the special man she has chosen? A recognized rite of passage the young woman could look forward to and plan for, and not just something that happens one night before she has to sneak back into her house after curfew? Wouldn't that be a wonderful tradition?

But we already have that ritual in America-it's called a WEDDING.

Sex outside of a committed relationship is ultimately unfulfilling at the very least, and destructive at its worst. Not just for girls, but guys as well hurt themselves when they have sex with random partners, or even "girlfriends" they are not committed to. You should understand the power of sex and understand that it is nothing to take lightly. Sex is designed to be an expression of love, a sacred spiritual bond between two people. But it can't work that way if you try to use it outside of a committed relationship.

Yes, of course biologically speaking, sex is a reproductive function. You may say, "Sex is designed to propagate the species!" But humans give meaning to their actions. Consciousness is the unique gift that humans have. If houses were simply shelters like a bird's nest, or a Neanderthal's cave, why do we decorate them and create a home out of a building? If eating were simply a way to stay alive, why do we have feasts and gatherings at holidays, etc.? In the same way, sex is not just a way to reproduce. It has a greater meaning beyond that.

Sex is also not simply a thing that people can do for pleasure. Sex was not designed for strangers to get together and do it, just to "have fun." Sex is such a beautiful and holy act, it joins the body, heart, mind and soul all at once. When people abuse it, and do it with people they hardly know, it's no wonder they feel so sad and empty afterwards.

You were not born on this earth to live a meaningless existence, reproduce, and then die. You are a precious soul and you have a purpose on this earth. Your purpose is not to be used for someone's sexual pleasure, or to have your heart broken by a relationship gone wrong. You have a higher purpose in this life, and casual sex is one thing that can keep you from finding that purpose.

The heartbreak and misinformation that I see in my classroom every week motivated me to survey my former chemistry and biology students who are now seniors. The results of the survey both surprised me and didn't surprise me. I knew girls were hurting as a result of having had sex for the wrong reasons, with the wrong guys, at the wrong time. What I didn't realize was that no one was telling them the truth about sex. I wanted to get the message to them and to other girls that sex is sacred, and not to throw away your virginity and your heart in high school and hurt yourself. Some of the consequences can last for life.

So if sex is so sacred, why do people seem to do it all the time, so irreverently?

1. Everyone is NOT doing it, and
2. They don't know the important truth about sex, and they believe other things about sex that are not true.

## 1. Everyone is NOT doing it!

50% of senior girls surveyed are virgins. They have made it to age 17 or 18 without having sex and they are still breathing! And these are not unpopular or unattractive girls. I know because many of them were in my classes. Some of their comments about sex are:

- *"I've never cared about someone enough to do it, and I am still kinda young."*

- *"I'll have sex when I know that it's right, but it won't be for a LONG time!"*

- *"Why not wait on Mr. Right, go to the clinic, get him checked out, get married, then have sex?"*

- *"I have not had sex yet because I see no need to."*

- *"I plan to wait until I am married because sex is special and you should not do it with just anybody. It is not just a physical thing, you are giving a part of your soul to that person."*

- *"I can wait, and I am not just some freak!"*

- *"I believe sex is for marriage only."*

- *"I haven't found anyone worthy enough to give my virginity to."*

- *"Your body is your temple, take care of it."*

- *"My life is complicated enough without sex to make it even more hectic."*

Even a 1995 survey at UCLA showed that not ALL college students are "doing it" either. Almost 50% of UCLA undergraduates under 21 had never had intercourse (*source-Daily Bruin online*).

So if sex is supposed to be sacred, why do girls enter into it so casually? Because they believe other things about sex, and no one has told them what is true about sex. It breaks my heart and amazes me that there is such a lack of truthful advice for young women today. Not sex education, or encouragement to have "safe sex," but the fact that few people tell teens that *casual* sex is destructive to relationships and to their hearts and souls.

One day after class I found a note that had been carelessly left under a desk. One sophomore student had written to the other that a guy she had had sex with denied ever even touching her that weekend, and she wrote that she was very worried because her period was late. How heartbreaking for this girl to realize that he didn't even care about her enough to admit that they had been together. When I found that note, I realized that many girls do not know the truth about sex.

What are some of the untrue beliefs that girls have about sex, or about themselves?

1. Sex is just something that people do
2. Sex is automatically part of being in love
3. Sex is a rite of passage for everyone, it's best just to get it over with
4. Sex is the final step of making out
5. Sex is something you have to do to keep a guy, especially older guys
6. Sex implies a special connection with or ownership of a guy
7. Sex and partying are just part of being a teenager
8. Sex means that you are desirable or attractive
9. Sex feels good, so why not do it?
10. Sex only includes sexual intercourse, not oral sex, etc.

Which of these beliefs do you have about sex?
Let's examine some of these beliefs to see how useful and sound they are to young women.

## Chapter 2-False Beliefs about Sex

### "Sex is just something that people do"

I think a lot of girls believe this one about sex. In fact, 66% of girls who have had sex said that they did because they felt like the time/person was right. In other words, they thought that they had reached that mysterious, elusive "right time for sex." A lot of magazines, movies, and even your friends will advise you that you'll know when the time is "right." The trouble is, you might feel like it's the right time to have sex, but what can seem right usually ends up not being the right thing afterwards. If sex is "just something that people do," something that doesn't really mean anything, then any time would be the "right" time, and any guy you were dating would do. But that's not what senior girls wrote on their surveys, based on their experiences:

- *"My first time was right after I turned 15, with a boyfriend of more than a year. The person was right, but the time wasn't."*

- *"I should have waited, but it's too late."*

- *"We had been together for more than 2 years, but I sorta regret doing the whole thing."*

- *"The first time I had sex it was a mistake because I thought I loved him, but I didn't."*

- *"He wasn't the right one and I felt pressured into it."*

- *"After an experience I knew I had made the wrong decision, and now I plan to wait."*

- *"I <u>was</u> in a relationship which involved sex. But that's over now."*

- *"I felt like the time/person was right. But I didn't think it through."*

- *"He was my best friend and I was curious. Now I regret it."*

All of these girls indicated on their survey forms that they had sex because they felt that the time/person was right. But every time, the time turned out not to be right after all.

When I was a sophomore in high school, my friends and I would talk about and wonder to ourselves, "Who do you think it's going to be?" We wondered who our First Time would be with. And nobody said anything about love. We just assumed that if we were going out with somebody, that future boyfriend would end up being The One we lost our virginity to. That seemed to be the way it worked. We saw the popular senior couples walking in the hallways holding hands. Everybody knew they were having sex. It really seemed romantic and dreamy, and we wanted that same fantasy relationship for ourselves.

As it turned out, one of my friends had already had sex with a much older guy. He was nowhere to be found by the time she was 16, and she spent the rest of her high school career making the same mistake over and over again. She dated a guy briefly, had sex with him, and he always ended up dumping her, or finding someone else.

Another one of my friends did seem to have that fantasy relationship. She had sex with her boyfriend who was a popular junior. But by the time we were juniors and he was a senior, she was sick of him, and she was relieved when they finally broke up and he went off to college.

Another of my friends also started going out with a popular junior guy that year. They probably had sex, although she never did talk about it to us. But her boyfriend broke up with her right before his senior year started. Apparently he and his friends had made some kind of fraternity pact to be single for their senior year, and to play touch football every Sunday in the park.

As for me, I didn't really date anyone until I was a senior. Then I fell madly in love with a much older guy (26!) and probably would have had sex with him if I could have figured out a way to get out of my house and find him on weekends. He actually ended up having to leave town quickly because he owed some cocaine dealers a lot of money. True story. I heard that he is married now and has two kids, but his wife was running around on him, so I don't know what his marital status is today.

So we all dreamed about that fantasy relationship, and we were all willing to include sex into that fantasy. We believed that sex is what you do when you have a serious boyfriend. But what never occurred to us is what happens AFTER that fantasy relationship is over, and all of the relationships did END.

In high school, you can get caught up in the fantasy. You

might think that you will eventually marry the guy you are dating. Admit it, how many times have you written your first name and his last name, just to see what it sounded like?

But the reality is, a lot happens after graduation. You will most likely not be getting married. If you really want to get married, try bringing it up to your boyfriend and see what kind of reaction you get. I doubt if he will be setting the date and rushing out to buy the ring.

So if you probably will not be marrying a guy you are dating in high school, why waste your virginity on it?

After graduation you will need time to experiment with different courses of your life, to try different careers, or majors, or jobs, or take classes at the community college, etc. And guys will need the same time to find out who they are, too. Marriage is a serious lifelong commitment, you will want to use the time you have when you are young and single to enjoy your independence and to carve out your direction in life.

Also, your taste in men can change a lot from when you're younger to the time when you're ready to get married. For example, in high school, your "type" might be jocks. Maybe you want to marry the guy in your school who has been recruited by a big college to play hockey for them. When you get to be about 20 or 21, you might be sick of going to all his games, supporting him when there's a losing streak, memorizing NHL statistics to impress him. The qualities that you look for in a guy could change a lot. You might want to look for a guy who has the time and the desire to be your personal cheerleader, instead of the other way around.

During high school, you might think the time has come for you to finally have sex. But the seniors who had sex because they thought the time was right wrote that it wasn't the right time after all. Even those girls with serious boyfriends wrote that. None of the girls wrote that they were glad that they had sex when they did. Saving sex for the right time and person, when you do get married, is one of the best decisions you can make for yourself.

## Chapter 3-False Beliefs about Sex

*"Sex is automatically part of love. Step 1, fall in love, Step 2, have sex."*

It's interesting to think about how deeply ingrained this belief is in our culture. I didn't even notice that I held this belief until I started writing this book. 60% of senior girls surveyed said that they had sex because they were in love. Period.

Now I would certainly argue that sex with love is superior to sex without love. But even having sex upon realizing that you love someone is NOT NECESSARILY the next logical step. It is absolutely a reasonable choice to love someone, and NOT have sex with that person. Have you ever thought about that?

Love makes a strong impetus for having sex, but

commitment is the only insurance you have against any of the results of sex. When you love someone, you are anxious to share in that feeling, and to experience new things together. Sometimes you might feel as if your heart will burst when you are in love, because the feelings fill you up and overwhelm you! Life is so wonderful, you never knew how wonderful until you fell in love. You want to dance and sing, and yes, you want to have sex!

But couldn't you put it off for a month, or a year, or years? Can you wait and see how your relationship develops, put in the time and work that it takes to make a relationship stronger and richer? Not that you'll never have sex with someone you love, but can you just <u>wait</u>? You could talk to each other more, learn more about each other, find out what his best memory is; have you ever seen him cry? How does he feel about abortion, religion, divorce? Would he cheat on you if he had the chance and he knew that you would never find out?

Take a day trip together, babysit your little sister together, play basketball. Have you ever been shopping together? Does he know your favorite movie, does he know what you want to do when you "grow up"? How many years have you spent Christmas together, have you EVER spent Christmas together? Do you know what he would like for his birthday? What did he get you for your birthday? There is so much to learn about each other. Having sex too soon in a relationship, even a loving relationship, can damage the important foundation that must be established first. How sad to be in a sexual relationship and realize, "We don't really have that much to say to each other."

One senior wrote, *"You think you love them and sex can mess up that "love"! It makes things a lot harder. I really did love my boyfriend and I thought I was ready, but after we had sex we broke up on and off-because of having sex! We never wanted to break up because we were each other's first. It was just really hard and a painful experience."*

Many girls have learned the hard way that having sex in a relationship before he is committed to you actually makes things WORSE. The relationship starts to revolve around sex. Every time you get together you have to have sex. You can't go back to the way it was before, and now there are all these things to worry about. You don't talk as much as you used to, you spend more time making arrangements to get together and have sex.

Emotions can be so strong, it's easy to get caught up in passion and set the course of the relationship towards sex. But if you can wait out that tidal wave of emotions you can avoid waking up the next day wondering who it was you have given yourself to, if you did the right thing, and if he truly loves you.

And while you certainly may love him, how do you <u>know</u> if he loves you, too? Some girls want to believe so badly that sex and love are the same thing, and that a guy must love her if he is having sex with her. Unfortunately, sex can mean no such thing. 60% of senior girls surveyed said they had sex because they were in love. But, a 1994 study showed that only 25% of men had sex for the first time because they felt affection for their partner. 51% of men had sex for the first time because they were curious or because they felt ready (Laumann et al).

That is a big difference between the sexes, and one that can cause a lot of pain and misunderstanding afterwards. The same survey showed that 12% of men had sex for the first time for physical pleasure, while only 2.8% of women did. It's strange to think of two people getting together under such paramount circumstances, each one thinking completely different things.

It's important to know that guys can be on different life schedules about relationships and love. Most guys want to establish themselves in a career before they settle down, and that may not be until their late 20s or 30s. If they had a choice between changing cities for a better job, and staying where their girlfriend was, they would be more likely to change cities. Girls, on the other hand, tend to put relationships first, and in the same situation, the girl would be more likely to turn down the job in order to stay with a potential husband.

The well-known verse about love that is read at most weddings comes from I Corinthians 13: *Love is patient, love is kind, and is not jealous; love does not brag and is not arrogant, rude, selfish, nor quick to take offense. Love keeps no score of wrongs, does not gloat over another's sins, but delights in truth. There is nothing love cannot face, there is no limit to its faith, its hope, and its endurance. But now abide faith, hope, and love, these three; but the greatest of these is love.*

Isn't that beautiful? When you are inclined to have sex because you love someone, remember that true love is patient and kind, not impatient and in a hurry to "go all the way." You can actually love someone <u>too</u> much to have sex with him, rather than feeling like you love him, so you want to have sex. In the same way, he should be patient, kind, and loving to you. That is <u>real</u> love. Not pressure or begging or selfishness. I think this experience from one of my favorite former students is particularly inspiring:

*"I have been in several horrible relationships and I have made huge mistakes. Now, I have been with my boyfriend for over a year and we both agree to wait until marriage. Not every guy is bad or a hornball. Because me and Jesse openly discuss "the topic," our relationship is the best I have ever had. From the very beginning we <u>both</u> said we did not want to have sex until we got married. It's wonderful to not feel pressured. But, from the very start we <u>both</u> made up our minds to wait!"*

## Chapter 4-False Beliefs about Sex

**"Sex is a rite of passage for everyone, it's best just to get it over with"**

23% of girls surveyed who had already had sex said that their FIRST TIME was *"with a guy I knew, but who was not a boyfriend."* One senior girl said, and I agree:

-*"I think that girls are having too much sex with random guys."*

If that many girls had sex with guys that they weren't even going out with, maybe they just wanted to hurry up and get their first time over with.

But you don't have to rush to lose your virginity or to "become a woman." The world is <u>not</u> divided into virgins and non-virgins. If you have not had sex yet, please don't be in a hurry to lose your virginity. Yes, you can get tired of not being able to participate in conversations about sex. If your girlfriends start whispering or laughing about different positions, or wild places they have done it, it can really make you feel left out to not have any wild or exciting stories to contribute. You can get tired of feeling like a baby. You might feel like a "goody-goody," or think that you are boring.

You do start to wonder what you're missing. Some of your friends might tell you sex is great. It certainly looks great on TV. What have you been waiting for, anyway?

BUT WAIT A MINUTE!! Please don't believe these lies about casual sex. We have already seen some of the real heartbreak that girls have felt about having sex. They would encourage you not to make the same mistakes and to avoid the emptiness of sex outside of a committed relationship. A senior wrote, *"It is not worth it to get hurt, pregnant, or an STD because you just wanted to get it over with."*

9% of senior girls who have had sex said that they had sex because they didn't want to feel left out or behind. And 10% of senior girls surveyed said that they feel way behind other girls in terms of "experience." I can understand that feeling, but I want to assure you, it's not a contest! One senior writes, *"You don't have to have sex to be popular. You can be popular by being friendly and outgoing to everyone around you."*

Show me where it is written that everyone should already have had sex by the time they're 18. And if they haven't, they are weird, or uncool, or whatever. I know many women in their 30s who abstain from sex until they are married. There's nothing wrong with these women. They are attractive, smart, and successful. One is a busy, outgoing financial analyst for a large semiconductor company. Another is a Claudia Schiffer lookalike who works as a civil engineer in Austin. Another is an insurance agent with exciting plans to go to Italy this summer. Another is busy in her second year of medical school. She is going to be a pediatrician. My older brother and his wife waited until they were married. Before they married, my brother's wife was a stunning Miss South Dakota in the Miss USA pageant. Today they have two beautiful children, and they are among one of the few couples that they know who are still together.

These women's lives do not revolve around men. They don't have trouble getting dates, and they don't subscribe to a "Cosmopolitan" vision of the single gal's life of casual sex and one-night stands. They don't sleep with a guy and then wonder the following week why he hasn't called, or wonder if he didn't like her for some reason, or if she said something wrong, or if he had a disease that she didn't know about. Waiting for a committed relationship does not banish you as a freak into the fringes of society. Even if you have a <u>long</u> wait, into your 20s or 30s, even!

Don't forget that there are plenty of guys who want to wait, too. Guys can be relieved when they don't have the pressure of having to get a girl in bed. They can slow down and get to know you, instead of having sex too soon.

## Chapter 5-False Beliefs about Sex

*"Once you are in a situation with a guy, you have to take it all the way. (or, sex is the final step of making out)."*

Again, this is another "rule" that is ingrained in a lot of girl's minds, but when we sit down and think about it, it's not logical at all. Where did this idea come from? Who ever said that once you start kissing and making out with a guy, you have to keep going from there?

However, it is true that once things start to heat up between a guy and a girl, it really is hard to stop. Sex is not the kind of thing you want to "just happen." One minute you can be making out with a guy, then he undoes your bra, tries to unzip your pants. You might not even want to say "no" when it gets to that point. You didn't plan on having sex, but you didn't try to avoid it, either. In fact, a survey showed that up to 25% of women did not even want to have their first time when it happened, although the sex was not actually forced (Laumann et al., 1994).

When you don't decide ahead of time what you are going to do when you're alone with a guy, you are pretty much deciding to have sex with him. In the heat of the moment it <u>is</u> difficult to turn back, and you might not want to, anyway. This is not to say that getting caught up in the heat of the moment is no one's responsibility. What I am saying is that if you don't decide ahead of time what you want to happen, you will end up in a situation without a plan. And then anything can, and usually does, happen. 51% of senior girls who have had sex said that their *first time* was something that was not planned, it was something that "just happened"!!!! Only 4 girls in the survey said that their first time was "something that I had planned for a long time." That is an incredible statistic to me. For most girls, there were no plans, no preparation. It "just happened" one night. One senior writes, *"My first time was with a boyfriend of more than two years. We never planned it or talked about it, it just happened one day."*

It's hard to turn back once you've started a heavy makeout session, not to mention the pressure a guy can put on you! "Come on, please?" he whispers in your ear, and you certainly don't want to ruin the moment. Some guys even get frustrated, mean, or angry if things don't go the way he wants them to. This should definitely be a red flag to you that something is wrong, and that you shouldn't go any further with this guy. Some other popular lines you might hear are, "Let's take our relationship to the next level." To which you can just answer, *"I think sex will ruin what we have going now, not make it better."*

"Explain why not. I don't understand."

*"I just don't want to."* (that's all the explanation you need to give)

"Maybe we should break up until you grow up."
*"Maybe we should break up until <u>you</u> grow up."* This is a great comeback that can really catch him off guard. Just the idea that you can do without him will make him think twice about pressuring you.

"You're going to wait until you're married?? I don't know if I'll ever get married."
*"That's too bad cause then you'll never get to have sex with me."*

"Of all the girls who like me, I picked you."
*"I think you have good taste."*

"I'm bored."
*"Only boring people get bored."*

"Why would you say no to pleasure?"
*"What makes you think you're that good?"*

"Just relax and let yourself go."
If you are tense or nervous, it's for a reason. Your mind and body are trying to tell you something. Respect your intuition and call things off. Tell him you will talk to him about it later. That will give you some time to think about it, and to decide what you really want to do, and what's best for you, and best for the relationship.

"Don't worry. I've got a condom"
*"I'm still not ready, condom or not."*

"You've had sex before/We've had sex before. What's the problem now?"

*"The problem is I did something I regret now. I don't want to go through that again."*

"This is boring!"
*"No kidding it's boring! I thought you would have more to talk about than sex."*

Sometimes a guy doesn't have to say a word to put pressure on you. He can say it all by what he is doing. Positioning your body where he wants it, leading you by the hand or by the waist to where he wants to go, ignoring what you're saying and continuing to kiss and touch and hold you. Again, in these situations, if you haven't already decided what you want to happen, you are setting yourself on a course to sex. I think that is what happens in a lot of situations. A girl hasn't thought about how far she wants to go, and she ends up in a situation where sex is almost inevitable. Here are some comments from girls who said that their first time "just happened":

-*"I think guys pressure girls into a lot of things that they don't want to do. It is OK to say "no," you have that right."*

-*"I wish I would have known when I was younger that "no" was okay. I could have seen right through that lying boy."*

-*"Was pressure from a guy an issue faced when going to have sex? I think if being alone with a guy you should be strong, mentally and physically, so that when you say "no" he or you don't change your mind for any reason."*

-*"Don't EVER do anything you don't wanna do."*

Remember that sex is meant to be a sacred bond between two people who are committed to each other. Save yourself the heartbreak of deciding to give away this precious gift in a few seconds because you have been swept away by lust, or because a guy is whining or putting pressure on you. Save yourself the heartbreak by deciding right now what you want to happen while you are in high school. Decide right now, as you are reading along, if you will have sex with a guy who has not committed to you. Decide if you will let him touch you below the waist, if you will be naked together, if you will perform oral sex on him, if you will touch him below the waist.

You know the saying, "Never go grocery shopping while you are hungry"? When you go to the grocery store while you're hungry, you end up pulling all the chips, candy, and high-fat foods off the shelf. But if you go to the grocery store when you're not hungry, you make better, healthier choices like lettuce for salads, apples, etc.

So in other words, make out your grocery list RIGHT NOW, before you're alone with that guy, so that you are not tempted to do more than what you are comfortable with while you are just sitting here reading a book. You might say, "But I don't even have a boyfriend!" Great!-An even better time to decide how far you want things to go when you do have one. A senior girl who could double for Tyra Banks writes, *"Most women seem to get pressured into it if they don't want to do it. Some are afraid of their mates. They need help about being strong and learning about the power of choice!"*

One caring senior girl wrote, *"Please describe the difference between love and lust so girls can understand the difference, and so girls won't do it just in the heat of the moment."*

| Love is: | Lust is: | Obsession is: |
| --- | --- | --- |
| Making sure he feels comfortable with your friends | Making sure you'll be alone together on the ski trip | Making sure he doesn't have Caller ID |
| Deciding to get to know each other better | Feeling like you can't stand it anymore-you have to have sex | Doing anything it takes to get and keep him |
| Listening to him tell the story about the game-winning catch for the 20th time | Fantasizing about having sex with him | Thinking about him constantly |
| Trusting that you'll be together if it's meant to be | Having sex every time you see each other | Driving by his house and stalking his workplace |

A senior cheerleader wrote, *"You really don't know what love is til you experience both lust and love."*

## Chapter 6-False Beliefs about Sex

### "Sex and partying are just part of high school"

Not true! Sex and drinking often do go hand in hand for some people. In fact, 13% of senior girls surveyed who have had sex had their FIRST TIME *at a party where they were drunk*!

It's sad to think of girls losing their virginity under these circumstances. And I <u>know</u> the girls wish their first time would have been more special.

The thing about drinking is that when someone feels the effects of alcohol, she is more likely to do more than what she normally would, with guys she normally wouldn't do things with. If that is the point of drinking, why even bother with him? In other words, if your judgment has to be impaired in order to go through with something, why are you doing it? It must not be a worthwhile thing to do if you wouldn't do it while you were sober.

Another "sobering" thing to think about is that the same is true for guys. You've heard the expression "beer goggles," right? If a guy is wearing "beer goggles," it means he sees a girl as being attractive because he is so drunk. Do you want to be the object of some guy's foggy, drunken gaze? If he would have sex with you when he's drunk and horny, but wouldn't touch you with a ten-foot pole when he's sober, that's pretty bad. Nothing to be proud of.

This particular belief about sex, that sex and partying are

just part of being a teenager, is probably the most dangerous. When someone has sex under the influence of alcohol, she is less likely to have the foresight to insist on using protection. How many unwanted pregnancies are the result of weekend bashes? How many girls contract a sexually transmitted disease one night after a drunken fumbling in somebody's parent's house?

When a girl has sex after drinking, she is also more likely to put herself in a situation that could escalate into physical violence, or even rape.

And most often, how many girls wake up the day after a drinking binge and cry because they have had sex with a guy they hardly know, and in the most degrading and irreverent circumstances?

What's sexy about throwing up on yourself, slurring your speech, not being able to walk, peeing your pants, crying inconsolably to everyone at a party? What's sexy about getting screwed, banged, nailed?

This brings up another question: what are teenage girls doing even drinking at all? Possession of alcohol under the age of 21 is illegal, but that hardly seems to have deterred America's youth. The classic reasoning is, "There's nothing else to do in this town." But I have heard young women who lived in <u>Austin</u> say that! There are always plenty of things to do-getting drunk and getting laid are NOT your only choices. One senior girl writes, *"People shouldn't be drinking anyway, who cares if you are 21? It is dumb! You don't have control over your body!"*

If you don't want to miss out on all the "fun," you can still go to the parties and be the designated driver. The down side to doing that is that you see how stupid everyone looks and acts when they are wasted. But you can still go if it makes you feel better, just know that you can still get in trouble for being in possession of alcohol if the party gets busted.

Other things you can do besides getting drunk are go to a concert or listen to a live band, go to a movie, GET A JOB, work out at the gym. Pursue your hobbies or interests. Do you want to work for the FBI when you get older-maybe you can intern at the police station. Do you want to run a day care center? Volunteer to work with little kids. There are lots of things you can do to make your life better or to help other people. Getting wasted is not one of them.

## Chapter 7-False Beliefs about Sex

### "Sex is something you have to do to keep a guy interested, especially older guys"

11% of senior girls surveyed who have had sex said that they had sex because they did not want to lose their boyfriends. I hope that seems as sad to you as it does to me, because you should recognize that sex is not a good strategy for hanging on to a guy. And if you have to come up with things to do to "hang on to him," that's a bad sign. One senior girl writes, *"If you have to have sex with a guy to keep him, then that guy is not right for you."*

Another senior says, *"If sex is all he's interested in, obviously he is not that interested in you."*

If it's getting to that point with a boyfriend, you would probably feel better and be able to get a fresh perspective if you took a little break. I don't mean break up, but do something to get a little distance from it all. Don't make this important decision while you're immersed in thoughts of him. Spend the weekend with girlfriends instead, visit relatives with your family or by yourself.

What is your hobby? Drawing, sports, writing, singing, taking pictures, movies, reading? When a relationship gets "serious," it's easy to lose track of other parts of your life. You can become consumed by thoughts of the relationship, obsessed by maintaining the relationship. Everything is about him, him, him.

You don't want to lose him, you see him as the light of your life, maybe the best thing that ever happened to you. If you start to feel this way, like your whole life is about your boyfriend, and making sure that you stay together, and making sure that he is happy, it is crucial for you to step back for a second and reevaluate the situation.

Are there other things you have done in order to hang on to him? Act a certain way, dress a certain way, drink, lie, pretend to like things that you don't like?

The irony of scrambling to hang on to a guy is that the harder you try, the more damage you do to the relationship. You can end up smothering him. Being who you think he wants you to be and doing what he wants you to do will not help you two stay together and it won't cause him to like you more.

It's not good for him to have a little child that he controls instead of a girlfriend. You are part of the relationship, so your opinions about sex and about what the two of you do together are very important. And it's not good for you to do things to appease him just so you can continue to see him. It will eventually backfire on him, and on you.

If the relationship has gotten to the point where he has said or implied that he will break up with you, find someone else, etc. if you don't have sex with him, then he is not cherishing and appreciating you. What he wants is sex, which is different than wanting you. And if you give it to him, you may indeed be able to extend the amount of time that you two go out. But what have you really gained? You may have postponed the inevitable for a week, or a month, but if the relationship came down to your "putting out" or not, what kind of Romeo is he? Why is it so important to him to have sex? Are his friends pressuring him into "scoring"? Does he feel like he's not cool because he's not "getting any"?

Actually, the opposite is true about sex and uncommitted relationships. Instead of being able to hang on to a guy, having sex usually hastens the end of the relationship. The guy can lose interest (if that's all he wanted in the first place). He can lose respect for you, it can cheapen the relationship if it happens too soon. You can start fighting about what the sex means to you, if it doesn't mean the same thing to him. You can start fighting about the amount of commitment he actually has to you. Sometimes he might regret having sex just as much as a girl because of the way it can mess up a developing relationship.

He can say he wants to take the relationship to the next level, or he can say that he really cares about you. If he wants to go to the next level, he can try writing you a poem, making a scrapbook of photos of the two of you, inviting you to spend more time with his family. Otherwise, he is just making up stuff that he thinks will convince you to have sex. If he truly does care about you and wants a way to show it, sex is not the way to go about it.

Let's switch the roles for a second to see if it makes more sense. Let's say you were dating a guy and you wanted him to buy you a car, and you <u>knew</u> he couldn't afford it. You told him that if he didn't buy you the car, then you would break up with him. Do you really like that guy, or do you just want the car?

It's the same thing with sex. If a guy is hinting around or putting pressure on you to have sex and you don't want to, then having sex with him isn't going to make him like you any more than you would like the guy buying the car for you. He likes the fact that he got what he wanted, but he doesn't suddenly think that you're a great person and want to be with you forever. It's ugly to think about that manipulating part of human nature, but it's imperative that girls not volunteer to be used for an immature guy's selfish wishes.

**OLDER GUYS**
This is particularly true with older guys. 29% of survey

participants who have already had sex said that their first time was with a guy who was over 18. I think this comment from one wisened senior girl says it all:

*"I made a huge mistake. I realize that now. I would advise girls not to date guys that are way older than them."*

Another senior writes, *"I dated an older guy and even though he never really said anything, I still felt pressured."*

Older guys (guys who are already out of school) can sometimes seem like a dream come true, can't they? There they are, (supposedly) living in the adult world. He probably has a car, and a job. He is more mature than the geeky guys in your classes who still think that punching you on the arm is a good way to flirt. And Older Guy has chosen you. It feels like such a privilege, such a high complement. Plus, if you want to escape the scene at your school, and be someone other than The Girl Who Sleeps in Biology Class, or Little Debbie Do-Right, or whatever, Older Guy doesn't know your school identity.

The thing is, what is Older Guy doing with high school girls? Why can't he find someone his own age? Older Guy has probably been around the block a few times, if you know what I mean. Older Guy might even have been married before, or still is married! (gross) One 17-year-old girl wrote about her experience with an older guy:

*"I once ran away from home because I thought it was the people in it who made me miserable, but boy was I wrong. When I was gone, 24-7 I was either stoned or on something. When I think of my first*

*so-called "great experience," all I can remember was his manhood forcefully on my innocence."*

And even if he truly is a Prince Charming and not a low-life loser dredging the high school for dates, are you prepared for the expectations that go along with dating him?   Already the relationship is off to an uneven start- he doesn't relate to your talking about classes, or grades, teachers, etc. Will he go to prom with you? It's not that you're "less" because you're younger, it's just that you are still in high school, that's all.

You know Older Guy is too old to go for this "let's wait until we're both ready" stuff about sex. He's already had sex, he's used to it by now. That doesn't mean that you have to go to his "adult" level. It means that if he's going to date YOU, he has to be prepared to operate on a high school level. Otherwise he should be dating other adult women. I know, I know, you don't want to lose him. But if the relationship has a future, then he should be able to wait for you. One senior girl wrote, *"One of my friends had an abortion because she had been with an older guy and she wasn't ready to be a mom."*

And, it sounds like the older guy probably wasn't ready to be a dad, either. In fact, <u>half or more</u> of all babies born to adolescent women in the United States are fathered by adult men (Landry & Forrest, 1995; Males & Chew, 1996)!

Not <u>all</u> older guys are sexual predators, but the majority of them shouldn't be trusted if they are pursuing girls in high school. If you are 14 and reading this book, I know that your Older Guy is a loser for sure. If you are 18 and reading this book, there's a chance that he might be a nice guy. One senior has a positive and reassuring experience with an older guy:

*"I have been seeing an older guy for a long time and my parents have full trust and faith in me. We both go to church and have our lives dedicated to God. He has told me he wants me to stay "pure" for him, and honestly, this to me isn't "puppy love." I would wait for him, like he waits for me. Hopefully, we will get*

*married."*

If you believe you can hang on to a guy by having sex with him, you may have convinced yourself that you are actually being generous and helpful to him. But while you are feeling like such a saint for giving all that you can to your man, he is wondering why you gave it up so easily. Contrary to those dreamy fantasies, he is <u>not</u> treasuring and cherishing you for this precious gift you can give. If this seems hard to believe, think about a guy you have known who was interested in you, but you had not committed to this guy. Have you ever had a guy calling you, talking to you, he told everyone he liked you, but you thought he was a geek and didn't want to go out with him? If he gave you gifts and made himself <u>completely</u> available to you, even though he knew you weren't committed to him, wouldn't you respect him even less? Wouldn't you see him as too eager? You certainly wouldn't fall madly in love with him because you knew he would do <u>anything</u> for you.

So don't expect a guy who is not committed to you to be grateful to you and to love you, just because you are giving a lot of yourself to him. Can you imagine a guy saying to his friends, "Stefanie is really special, she gives me sex whenever I need it"?? Or, "I know that Stefanie <u>truly</u> cares about me because she had sex with me."??? <u>Please</u>. Having sex with a guy who is not committed to you does not make him think that you are his special angel, or that you are "the best girlfriend there ever was."

Remember that sex can mean something different to a guy. He might think it means that he is manly, or a stud, or whatever. He may be bragging about "getting play" to his friends. Meanwhile you are drawing his name in little hearts on your notebook. To him, it's just sex. To you, it's a big part of yourself, and part of your soul. Don't give it to someone who can't appreciate the powerful act that it is. And don't ever use sex to hang on to a guy, especially older guys. It won't work.

## Chapter 8-False Beliefs about Sex

### "Sex implies a special connection with a guy, or ownership of a guy"

Recently I heard a senior guy in one of my classes trying to describe an acquaintance to his guy friends. He said, "You know Brandi, she messes with Blake sometimes." The guys thought about it for a moment, and nodded. Yes, they did know who Brandi was.

Can you imagine this Brandi hearing the conversation? She didn't even make it to the level of "Blake's girlfriend"! Apparently, Blake isn't interested in a relationship, but he can get physical affection from Brandi whenever he needs to. And, apparently, Brandi doesn't respect herself enough to expect kind and loving treatment from Blake. She just gives it up whenever Blake comes around. She probably gets mad and throws a fit when she can't get him to call her regularly, or go out with her. It's not a big mystery what the problem is here.

I hope Brandi doesn't think that it's a good strategy to sleep with a guy to become his girlfriend, or even just to be associated with him. Sex does not mean that you have a special connection to a guy. He is not obligated to you because you had sex with him. It seems that he should be, but don't learn the hard way that a guy who is not committed to you in the first place won't change his mind after you have sex with him.

Have you ever seen those trashy talk shows where two girls are fighting over some loser guy? One girl says, "He's mine!" The other girl says, "No, he's going home with me!" Both girls seem to think that because he had sex with her, that the guy is "with" her. Neither girl wins because the guy can walk away. Of course he should feel guilty about what he has done, but it never would have happened if the girl had not thought that the guy was her man just because she had sex with him.

One senior wrote, *"When I changed schools I didn't know anyone and I thought that by sleeping with guys I might meet more people. But I now regret doing all of it."*

That's why it's so important to have the commitment from the guy. Otherwise he can just walk away, and a girl is left with a lot of shattered dreams. IT HAPPENS EVERY DAY. Going out, being serious, wearing his class ring, any gifts or promises he has made, having sex, living together, having a man's baby, all these things do not mean that you have a claim on a guy. Living together just means that the guy gets to put off getting married. He doesn't have to make a commitment because living together is what the girl is settling for.

Marriage is the only guarantee that a guy intends to be there the day after. Living together is not a commitment, it's just sharing living space and the rent.  Did you know that couples who live together before marriage have an 80% higher chance of divorcing than couples who do not live together before marriage??? (Bennett, Yale Univ., 1988)

Actually, NOT having sex with him can be more strengthening to the relationship than having sex.  If you want to have a truly special connection with a guy, get to know him better, and wait for a mutual commitment to have sex.  It might be a totally new revelation to him.  He most likely would think, "Wow! This girl is *different* than other girls I've been out with before. Maybe we really have a future together."

## Chapter 9-False Beliefs about Sex

### *"Sex means that you are desirable or attractive"*

No, having sex definitely doesn't mean that you are "all that." Anyone can have sex, it takes wisdom and a peaceful patience to not have sex. I hate to put this quote in here, but I feel like it's important for young women to know. I know when I heard it at age 16, it certainly was an eye-opener for me: "Pussy's pussy, you don't f*ck their face." In high school, one of my girlfriends told me that her boyfriend's friends said that. I was surprised, but it did explain that the way girls view sex can be <u>much</u> different than the way (some) guys view sex.

One time I was getting a haircut at the salon when the husband of the stylist's friend called my stylist. The husband was asking the stylist if she knew of any other guys that his wife had been with. Apparently, this friend met some guy over the internet and had been having an affair. I asked my stylist why she thought her friend was doing that. She said that her friend probably wanted the attention from men. I was surprised that a woman in her 30s could think that sex was a good way to get love, affection, attention. Then it occurred to me that she must have thought that in high school, and she STILL hadn't learned that it wasn't true. Don't be this sad woman-not now, and not when you're older.

It's easy to think that if a guy wants to have sex with you, it means he thinks you're really pretty, hot, sexy, or whatever. The truth is that while you may indeed be very attractive, a guy can want to have sex just because it's sex, not because you are so beautiful he wants you in particular. Every girl loves to get attention from guys, who wouldn't want to hear that you look great in a certain shirt, or that your hair is a big turn-on, or those jeans make your butt look good? But that doesn't mean that you have to return the complement by having sex. You don't owe a guy anything because he admires your looks. He can <u>look</u> all he wants, right? As long as you feel comfortable with it.

AND, more importantly, don't feel that if you <u>aren't</u> having sex, you must therefore be <u>un</u>attractive. Seeing all the attention that the homecoming queen gets could make you feel inferior. But just because you're not 5' 10", perfectly thin with a 36" bust and 24" waist doesn't mean that you're unattractive. There are lots of different ways of being attractive. The homecoming queen or Britney Spears or whoever are not the only versions of attractive. Different girls have different attractive features. One curvy girl could be attractive because she is voluptuous, and a skinny girl can be attractive in a svelte, cool way. Girls can be attractive in different ways: pretty, cute, classically beautiful like Gwyneth Paltrow, or warmly attractive like Jennifer Love Hewitt. Attractive can mean curvy like Jennifer Lopez, or athletic like Gabrielle Reese, or sensuous like Liv Tyler, or unique like Leelee Sobieski. And I couldn't leave out a discussion of attractiveness without mentioning Tina Turner-she's 60 and she still looks that good!

You should know that you are attractive in a certain way, and don't fall for the first guy who tells you so. It was true before he said it, and you don't owe him sex or anything else for noticing.

## Chapter 10-False Beliefs about Sex

### "If it feels good, do it!"

A lot of things feel good, but that doesn't mean that life is all about doing them. It can feel good to eat a whole gallon of chocolate ice cream, too, for a while. Drugs can make you feel good temporarily, but we all know that doing them isn't good for you.

34% of girls who have had sex checked "*I wanted to see what it was like*" on their survey forms. The ironic thing is that sex is supposed to feel good-they do seem to be moaning and groaning a lot when they do it on TV. But in reality, as a young woman it probably WON'T feel that good to you. Eventually, of course, you and your husband can work your way up to a great sex life. But right now while you are young, inexperienced, stressed about a boyfriend or about getting pregnant, getting caught, etc., sex will not feel that good.

In fact, one girl even volunteered the information on her survey that, *"My first time was boring."* Another disenchanted senior wrote, *"From what I have heard, it is not that great, marriage or not."* Don't be discouraged by this, just be reassured that when you don't feel lightning and thunder the first time, (in the future), that's pretty normal. Things will definitely improve eventually.

And just to break the suspense of what it feels like the first time, I'll tell you: it feels like someone laying on you, putting something in your vagina.

## Chapter 11-False Beliefs about Sex

### *"Sex only includes sexual intercourse, oral sex, etc. doesn't count"*

Just try telling that to your future husband. "But I never had sex with those guys, I only gave them blow jobs." He will not be comforted.

Although you cannot get pregnant from oral, anal, or manual sex, you can still get sexually transmitted diseases through these acts. In fact, in one region of Georgia a health-screening project among middle school students intended to detect meningitis bacteria in the throat found that several girls had pharyngeal gonorrhea (New York Times on the Web, December 19, 2000).

And regardless of what your friends tell you, they are still sex, thus the name, "oral sex," etc. Anything involving contact with the genitals is sex! There is a lot of confusion about what constitutes sex. Many young people believe that vaginal intercourse is sex, and any other sexual behaviors are not sex. A 2000 study published in Family Planning Perspectives reported that 55% of 15 to 19 year old boys said they had had vaginal intercourse, but 67% said they had experience with other sexual behaviors. More than 1 in 10 boys had engaged in anal sex, half had received oral sex from a girl, and about 33% had performed oral sex on a girl.

No, I'm not trying to rain on your parade if you feel like you found a way to technically stay a virgin. It's just that the effects on an uncommitted relationship of other forms of sex are the same as for sexual intercourse. What do you get out of it if you give a guy a blow job or a hand job? He can walk away, break up with you, things can change, and you're still left with nothing but lost respect and regret. It's still embarrassing to see him in the hallways afterwards, and it still leaves you feeling sort of empty and used, just like sexual intercourse in an uncommitted relationship.

If you are in the majority of teenage girls who have not had sex yet, hopefully you aren't feeling left out. You're doing great so far! Don't feel that there's something wrong with you. Remember, 74% of the girls who have had sex regret experiences they have had.

Even after reading this, you might still be thinking, "Do you seriously expect me to wait until <u>marriage</u>?" And my answer is "Absolutely!" Sex can be destructive to an uncommitted relationship. Do you want to have a mediocre relationship where the threat of breaking up looms every day, or do you want an awesome, incredible relationship with a closeness and friendship you have <u>never</u> experienced before? I'm <u>guaranteeing</u> you that if you allow the relationship to develop slowly and steadily, and keep the sex out of it, you are on your way toward forming a rock solid bond between you and your future husband that you can have confidence in when you walk down that aisle. One senior girl writes, *"I am not waiting to have sex until I am married because I feel that sex is an important part of marriage. What if you marry a guy and the sex is awful? Not just the first time, but always?"*

I understand her concerns but I want to reassure her that sex with someone you love can never be AWFUL.  Also, if you slept with a guy before you were married, and then you decided you didn't like having sex with him, would you break up with him because of it?  Would you trade in your fiancee for someone who was more studly in the sack??

Yes, sex is an important part of marriage, but you can relax when you're married and work together at your sexual relationship. You undoubtedly can talk to your husband about what you like and don't like in bed because you have already established good communication between the two of you.  Hopefully you have become the best of friends, so you will naturally learn about each other's bodies after you're married.  Your sexual relationship will grow and develop as the years go by.

You can also get a pretty good idea of what sex will be like with your future husband by measuring the amount of passion and intensity in his kisses.  And one senior girl writes: *"If you are married then you know they will be there for you after the deed is done."*

If you have had sex and you regret it, don't feel hopeless.  There is hope and a bright future there for you.  No, you can't take back the past, but you <u>can</u> change how you will live your life in the future. The good news is that, with enough time and healing, you can restore your virginity, spiritually.  Wait for your husband, and when you make love for the first time, it will feel like a brand new experience.

*Chapter 12*

*A Girl Who Got Pregnant Tells Her Story*

Despite public service campaigns and sex education in schools, most teenagers who do have sex do not use contraceptives consistently or effectively (Orr et al. 1992, Seidman & Rieder, 1994). Many teenagers do not use any contraception at all the first few times they have sex, and only a small percent always use some method of birth control (Braverman & Strasburger, 1993; Poppen, 1994). Even teenage couples involved in monogamous relationships where they have actually talked about contraception only use birth control some of the time, not all of the time (Pleck et al., 1993; Polit-O'Hara & Kahn, 1985).

Some couples rely on withdrawal (pulling out) as a method of birth control. Not only does this not protect from sexually transmitted diseases, it is not effective in preventing pregnancy. Approximately 19 out of 100 women whose partners use withdrawal as birth control still become pregnant within a year (Hatcher et al., 1994).

A lot of young women do not use birth control because they think that if they use birth control, it means they are planning to have sex. They would rather think that they just get caught up in the heat of the moment, and it happens.

If you are in a sexual relationship right now, I urge you not to necessarily get on the pill, but instead to listen to that little voice inside of you. The voice that is saying, "Maybe this isn't the best thing for me now." You can hear that voice because it whispers to you before you have sex, and you have to shut it off to go through with everything.

A lot of parents have the policy that if their daughter decides she is ready, they will go to the doctor or clinic and get her on the pill. However, this implies that the thing that they are most scared of is the girl getting pregnant. There are still diseases to contend with, and hearts can still be broken so easily. Sex in high school, when the relationship is uncommitted for the long term, is usually not the best decision for the girl and the guy. One senior girl writes about a friend:

*"I have a really close friend who had been going out with her boyfriend since 8th grade and last year she got pregnant and had a kid. They are still together, but her boyfriend is not as mature about the situation as her. She grew up, but he didn't. He goes out and parties while she stays home taking care of the baby."*

I had a student in my chemistry class last year who was pregnant. Shyan is a very honest, outgoing, and friendly 18-year old. Today she is married to her baby's father, and they are working hard to establish a life for themselves and little Noah. Shyan generously wrote her story to add to this book.

Shyan's story-"*My Experience with Teenage Sex*"

When I was in the eighth grade my best friend was always having sex. When I would spend the night with her she would leave me at her house while she went and had sex with her boyfriend. She used to tell me, "You have no idea what you're missing out on." At first I didn't care because all the guys still liked me. Then after a while the guys would suddenly take interest in my best friend. One of my guy friends told me when I asked him about it, "It's because she slept with them."

So one night I did what she had been doing all along, I had sex. But it wasn't with anyone special. And it is totally true that once the guy gets what he wants then he moves on to the next victim. No, guys aren't always the bad ones. My best friend that year, she seduced the guys and it was all because she wanted the attention. She couldn't stand the fact that the guys liked me and I didn't even have to wear a low-cut shirt.

At the age of 14 my best friend became a mom. That's when we quit being friends, when she found out she was pregnant.

A year went by before I engaged in any sexual intercourse and after that it was 9 months later before I had sex. I was not very sexually active.

My sophomore year in high school is when I met Zac. We were together for 3 months before we engaged in sexual intercourse. With this guy it wasn't just sex, it was much more. Seven months after we had been together, I found out I was pregnant. The whole time we were having sex, I always thought, "Well, it could never happen to me." Sure enough, the summer before my junior year I found out I was pregnant. A lot of people ask how I told my parents, but I think I got an easy break. My mom has real strong motherly instincts and one day she asked me if I was pregnant. I said I didn't know and she went and bought a test to confirm it. I didn't know how to handle the situation. I had so much going for me in school. I was a straight 'A' student and I was looking forward to going away to a good college. I threw that away for sex.

So I started in my regular school my junior year. I hid it really well for a while, but then my stomach started getting bigger and bigger and it became very clear that I was pregnant.

I knew people would talk about me. Once in a while, I would overhear them. That didn't really bother me, and that's what really surprised everyone. The way I looked at it was, if I was walking through the hallways, pregnant, everyone would know that IT CAN HAPPEN TO YOU, and maybe they would think about it before they engage in sex.

I do agree that sex is made for when two people fall in love, and that you should wait for that one person before you just let it happen. It's taken a lot for me to see it that way, but I do now. With girls it's different than with guys. Did you know that guys can be in a relationship where they never talk with their girlfriend, they just have sex? It's happening all around us. There are guys who say, "I love you" just to see if they would have a chance to get laid. A guy can tell a girl that it's his first time, that he's a virgin, but how do you know whether or not they actually are? Guys can tell when a girl is a virgin, it's a little hard to hide it. And most guys have no remorse when they take your virginity and dump you. Take that to heart before you consider losing your virginity with some guy.

Now being pregnant at the age of 16 was not my idea of fun. My friends all had different boyfriends all the time and always had guys flirting with them while I was getting stretch marks and cravings. My friends went to parties and I stayed home and read baby names out of a book. My friends bought new outfits, CD's and shoes while I bought baby clothes, toys and diapers. And let's not forget my monthly doctor visits. So my friends grew distant while I grew up.

My second semester of what was supposed to be my junior year, I transferred to a school called the Teen Parent Center. There I met a lot of girls who were fixing to be parents or who had just become parents. I became friends with a lot of those girls because we had a lot in common. One of my friends named Megan was 14 and expecting. The ages varied. TPC only took 7th through 12th grades and believe it or not, there was a homebound student that was in the 6th grade who was pregnant. Can you imagine being in elementary school and getting pregnant? We had a bunch of 7th and 8th graders that were pregnant. It's a sad thing.

Then one day my baby decides it's time to come into this world. I was in labor for 15 hours, can you imagine all that pain after 2 minutes of sex? Unfortunately, I had complications and I had to have a C-section. So on top of stretch marks, gained weight and a baby, I now have this big scar across the bottom of my stomach. Do you know how much it costs to have a baby nowadays? It cost me right around $15,000.

I'm not going to tell you not to have sex until you're married or at least out of school, or never have sex. I'm trying to tell you the consequences of having sex. Sex is not a bad thing once you're completely ready for sex and the consequences of having sex. My mom always asks my husband, "What's cheaper, a box of condoms or a baby?"

*Chapter 13*

## SEXUALLY TRANSMITTED DISEASES

*"I got herpes from my ex-boyfriend. When I told him, he actually accused me of giving it to him. But I know he gave it to me because he has been with a lot of scummy girls, and I have only been with one other guy and we used condoms. The worst part about herpes is that it never goes away. I get sores "down there" around the time of my period, and they last for a week. We are not even together anymore, it was so not worth it."*

Unfortunately, this young woman is not the only one. Each year, 3 million teenagers are infected with a sexually transmitted disease (Alan Guttmacher Institute, 1994). In a single act of unprotected sex with an infected partner, a teenage girl has a 1% risk of acquiring HIV, a 30% risk of getting genital herpes, and a 50%

chance of contracting gonorrhea! (Alan Guttmacher Institute, 1994)
Have you heard the saying, "When you have sex with someone, you are having sex with everyone they had sex with, too"? That can add up to a lot of people, even if it is only your first time.

One haunting example that moved me to write this book is the story of a group of kids in Conyers, Georgia. In 1996 over 200 young people were exposed to syphilis by having group sex or sequential sex with each other (Rothenberg et al., 1998). Many of the girls involved were under 16, and most of the time they had these group activities with some older guys that came over when the girls' parents were out for the evening. In that case, every girl or boy involved either had sex with someone who was infected with syphilis, or had sex with someone who had had sex with someone else infected with syphilis.

I hoped when I heard about this story that it was an isolated incident, but that is probably just denial. What were these young people searching for in their lives that they thought sex could satisfy? Thrills? Feeling like they belonged? Feeling like adults or like they were cool or desired? They may indeed have experienced all those things at the time, but a few months later, all they had to show for it was a sexually transmitted disease.

You might say that the answer to this problem is simply to wear condoms. However, we have already seen in the last chapter that most young people do not use condoms because they do not plan to have sex. It usually "just happens." When sex "just happens" one night, diseases can "just happen," and many of them cannot be cured.

Herpes, genital warts, hepatitis and AIDS <u>do</u> <u>not</u> <u>have</u> <u>cures</u>. If you got these diseases, you could not simply go to the doctor, get some pills or a shot and get rid of the disease. You would have these diseases <u>for</u> <u>life</u>.

Also, some diseases cannot be prevented even by using a condom. Herpes, genital warts, pubic lice and scabies can still be spread even when there is a condom used.

Condoms are no guarantee against pregnancy or any diseases, either. They can break or slip off. A 1995 study showed that more than 1 out of 10 women who use condoms as their only method of birth control become pregnant in one year's time (Post & Botkin). In other words, condoms are not 100% effective. You can't count on them to protect you.

There are other diseases you could get without even knowing you had them at first. **Chlamydia** is the most common bacterial sexually transmitted disease in the United States (Centers for Disease Control, 1997), and women who have it may not show any symptoms. Chlamydia is the most common cause of *pelvic inflammatory disease*, which results in chronic pelvic pain, fever, vomiting and ultimately, infertility. Even after it has been treated the scar tissue in the fallopian tubes leaves some women sterile (unable to conceive a child). Sexually active teenagers have higher infection rates of chlamydia than any other age group (Shafer, 1997), and young women who use birth control pills are at even higher risk of getting chlamydia (Ivey, 1997).

**Gonorrhea** (also known as "the clap") is another sexually transmitted disease that you could have without knowing it. There may not be any symptoms until it has progressed considerably. Like chlamydia, gonorrhea causes *pelvic inflammatory disease* (PID). PID can cause ovary and uterus tissue to grow together, causing severe pain when a woman has sex, or even walks or stands. Gonorrhea rates are exceptionally high among teenagers and young adults, much higher than rates among people in their 30s and 40s (Crooks & Baur, 1999). Men may not show any symptoms of infection, so it's not like you could tell by looking at them whether they have gonorrhea or chlamydia.

**Syphilis** is a potentially fatal sexually transmitted disease. It first appears as a sore on the body at the site of the infection. It can be transmitted through oral sex as well as vaginal intercourse. After a month, if the disease is left untreated, a skin rash appears on the body, usually on the soles of the feet and palms. If the syphilis is still not detected or treated, it can result in heart failure, blindness, paralysis, and liver damage (Moran, 1997).

**Genital herpes** is another disease that men can have without showing any symptoms. It is so widespread, health authorities have stated that people "who have unprotected contact with multiple partners should know that unsuspected exposure to herpes is virtually <u>guaranteed</u>" (Arvin & Prober, 1997).

Herpes causes painful blisters to form on the genitals, and an infected person can experience repeated outbreaks of the blisters over the course of their life. Currently there is no cure for herpes, although there are medications that can shorten the length of time that an outbreak lasts. Herpes can be transmitted from an infected person to another during any type of sexual contact (oral sex, intercourse, anal sex), even if the infected person does not currently have an outbreak of the blisters. Two very serious complications of herpes in women are an increased risk of getting cervical cancer, and transmitting the virus to newborns through the birth canal. Pregnant women who have herpes may be advised to deliver the baby by cesarean section.

**Genital warts** is what it sounds like: warts on the genitals. Like herpes, it is caused by a virus, and like herpes, you could get it from someone who does not show any symptoms. The warts typically appear around 3 months after contact with an infected person. They can be treated by freezing them off with liquid nitrogen. Large warts may have to be vaporized by laser or surgically removed. Even after that, the warts can come back because the virus that causes them stays in the body, and there are currently no cures for the virus.

**Pubic lice** (crabs) are also what they sound like-lice in the pubic area. Pubic lice are large enough to actually be *seen* crawling around with the naked eye (gross)! A pubic louse grips a pubic hair with its claws and sticks its head into the skin, where it feeds on blood from tiny blood vessels (Crooks & Baur, 1999).

They can be transmitted without having sex, if two people bring their pubic areas together, or by sleeping on infected bedsheets, or from wearing infested underwear.

In the United States, **AIDS** is the second leading cause of death, after accidents, among persons ages 25-44 (Centers for Disease Control, 1997). In addition, it is easier for a woman to get AIDS from a man than it is for a man to get AIDS from an infected woman. Teenagers currently have one of the fastest growing rates of infection because they tend not to use condoms, and to have multiple partners.

Remember that when you have sex with someone, you are also having sex with everyone they have had sex with. Even if you know who a guy has been with, you don't know the partners of the girls he was with. And their partners, and their partners, and so on. Also, some diseases may be transmitted through unwanted sexual contact, such as abuse or rape. The network of people you could be sleeping with by sleeping with just one guy can include hundreds of people that you don't even know, and people from cities far away from yours.

A virus does not discriminate, it infects regardless of who you are. A bacteria will spread, even if you are a "nice girl," the homecoming queen, even if you and your boyfriend are "in love," even if his former girlfriend is no longer around.

Yes, it is scary, but it's not like you have to have sex and take your chances. You can cuddle and kiss and hold hands and hug and you won't be missing out! You can take the time to develop a relationship, talk, get to know each other, go to the movies, go out to eat. There are tons of things to do with each other that are fun that DON'T involve sexually transmitted diseases!

Chapter 14

## SEXUAL ABUSE AND RAPE

*"I have a friend who told me recently that her dad sexually abused her when her parents were still married. She went through a time when she was hospitalized for depression, but I didn't understand what was wrong until now. I don't think she is completely over it because she is working as a topless dancer in a bar."*

Child sexual abuse is defined as an adult engaging in sexual contact of any kind with a child (Crooks & Baur, 1999). Although this topic may seem unrelated to the subject of this book, I have included it because it is shockingly common. Statistics about sexual abuse are difficult to gather, but one survey estimated that approximately 22% of women had been sexually abused as children (Gorey & Leslie, 1997). That means that thousands of girls today have been touched inappropriately, molested, or manipulated by a father, stepfather, uncle, or other man known to them. There is probably a girl in one of your classes who has been sexually abused.

Sexual abuse can be any behavior between a child and an adult that must be kept secret. It includes an adult using tricks, threats, power, or violence to have sexual contact with a child. For example, showing a child pornographic materials, being sexual in front of a child, and photographing a child for sexual purposes all constitute sexual abuse (McMullen, UMKC).

Young women who have been sexually abused experience extremely traumatic effects. They may find it difficult to form relationships, experience sexual dysfunction when they get married, low self-esteem, and depression. They are more likely to turn to drugs, alcohol, or food to medicate their pain. They are also at increased risk of being suicidal, and to being repeatedly victimized in other ways (Goodman & Fallott, 1998).

If you have been a victim of sexual abuse, you can call the Rape Abuse and Incest National Network hotline at 1-800-656-HOPE (1-800-656-4673). They have free 24-hour confidential counseling, and you can call even if an attack or incident occurred many years before. Their website is **www.rainn.org**


## SEXUAL ASSAULT AND RAPE

One girl wrote, *"I have a friend that really trusted a friend of hers, she had no reason not to. They weren't going out, they were just good friends. One day everyone was watching movies at his house. They all left to do something. She started to feel uncomfortable, and she should have: he pinned her down and raped her."*

Another senior wrote, *"When I was a junior I went out with my friends one night and we saw some people we know in this parking lot. So we parked and got out. While we were talking this senior guy stopped and so we started talking to him. I like trucks and he has a nice one so I wanted to ride in it. So I asked him and he said, "sure." I didn't realize that he was drinking beer til I got in. He was only going to take me around the drag once, but then he parked, turned the lights off, and locked the doors. I was so scared, I asked him repeatedly to take me back and he wouldn't. He tried to get me to do a lot of things but I didn't. I finally got away and he took me back to my friends. When I got back my friends asked me where I had been and the whole time I was telling them and crying he was sitting over in his truck laughing."*

Unfortunately, there are many women who have been raped or sexually assaulted. Again, the statistics are difficult to obtain because many women do not report the crime. Different studies have shown that the percent of women in America who have been raped or attacked is between 19% and 25% (Crooks & Baur, 1999).

Most rapes are committed by someone that the girl knows, not by strangers. Some men even think that rape is OK if he has been "led on." Rape is NEVER OK! Do not ever feel that a rape was your fault for any reason! If you have been raped, you can call a rape crisis center in your town, or the RAINN number (1-800-656-4673), and they can give you information about where to go in your town. If you have a friend who has been raped, be supportive and assure her that she is not responsible for the rape in any way.

*"Men are from Earth.  Women are from Earth.  Deal with it."*

-Betty Friedan

*Chapter 15*

*The Same Goes for Guys, too!*

This book is written for young women, but <u>every</u> <u>bit</u> of advice is true for guys as well.  Sex is designed to be a beautiful sacred bond between a man and woman who are committed to each other, and when guys use sex for reasons besides that, in situations where they do not care about the girl, they are hurting themselves as well as the girl.  It's never good for a guy's heart when he takes advantage of someone, and when he enters into sex without considering the girl's feelings.

One pretty and athletic senior girl writes, *"I believe there are many guys who are waiting for the right one and if both the guy and girl are virgins when they marry then it supports and sets an example of true love and purity."*

If you sit down and talk to guys, you will find that many of them would appreciate waiting, too. But the male culture encourages guys to "go for it" without regard to their feelings or to the girl's feelings. Their culture pushes them to be sexually experienced, with many girls. If you take this pressure off him by waiting until you are both committed, it can be a relief to him, and it's the best thing for you and for the relationship.

The effects on men of sex without commitment are just as damaging as they are to women. Guys can feel empty and depressed after a meaningless sexual encounter with a girl, just the same way that girls do. Most of the time, no one has told guys the truth about sex, either.

Also, pornography, strip clubs, one-night stands, and phone sex lines, etc. are not edifying to a man's spirit. They only desensitize him to his feelings and to women. In fact, repeated exposure to hardcore pornography has been proven to cause men to devalue the importance of monogamy, and lack confidence in marriage as an institution. Continued use of pornography also caused men in a study to become more callous towards women, and to develop an appetite for more deviant and violent types of pornography; normal sex no longer seemed to "do the job" (Zillman & Bryant, 1988).

Sexual addiction is one of the most widespread afflictions in the United States. Men can have a compulsion to have sex in the same way that there are addictions to gambling, overeating, bulimia. Men with sexual addictions use sex like a drug, to make themselves feel better. Sexual addiction is a devastating condition- it hurts the addict, his family, and all the partners he uses to satisfy the addiction. There are 12-step programs and SA groups to help a man with recovery, but the most difficult part is usually for the man to acknowledge that he has a problem. Our culture reinforces men who have many sexual partners.

Some of the signs of addiction include sexual behavior that has become out of control, and inability to stop despite severe consequences-including arrests, divorce, and losing a job. Other signs are sexual obsession and fantasy as a coping strategy, and excessive amounts of time spent in obtaining sex, being sexual. Another sign is neglect of important social or occupational activities because of sexual behavior (Carnes, *Don't Call It Love*, 1991).

When the addict uses sex for its adrenalin high, he is abusing sex, and taking advantage of someone else. That's why it's such a painful addiction. If you have questions about sexual addiction, you can visit the website of Sex Addicts Anonymous at **www.sexaa.org** or the website of Heart to Heart Counseling in Colorado Springs: **www.sexaddict.com** They offer phone counseling as well, the number is 719-278-3708.

But sex addiction is not the only way that casual sex can hurt a guy. I think this 15-year old boy's comment echoes the same feelings that a lot of guys have about sex, "Sometimes I think the whole world is too focused on sex. There are nights when I'm locked away in my girlfriend's bedroom while her parents are out, and I know it's her turn to give me a blow job because I went down on her the night before, but sometimes I think maybe we should really be out doing something else besides sex" (Salon.com, Dec, 2000).

About the Author

Kristen Anderson is a high school chemistry teacher in Texas. She grew up in Iowa, and graduated from Colorado College in 1993. She welcomes comments and questions from readers. You can e-mail her at **kristenaa@msn.com**

## BIBLIOGRAPHY

Arvin, A., & Prober, C. (1997). Herpes simplex virus type 2-A persistent problem. *New England Journal of Medicine*, 337, 1158-1159.

Braverman, P., & Strasburger, V. (1994). Sexually transmitted diseases. *Clinical Pediatrics*, January, 26-37.

Carnes, P., (1991). *Don't Call It Love*. Bantam Doubleday.

Centers for Disease Control (1997) Chlamydia trachomatis genital infections-United States, 1995. *Morbidity and Mortality Weekly Report*, 46, 193-199.

Centers for Disease Control (1997) AIDS rates. *Morbidity and Mortality Weekly Report*, 46, 165-173; 333-334.

Crooks, R., & Baur, K. (1999). *Our Sexuality*. Brooks/Cole Publishing Company.

Goodman, L., & Fallot, R. (1998). HIV risk behavior in poor urban women with serious mental disorders: Association with childhood physical and sexual abuse. *American Journal of Orthopsychiatry*, 68, 73-83.

Gorey, K., & Leslie, D. (1997). The prevalence of child sexual abuse: Integrative review adjustment for potential response and measurement biases. *Child Abuse & Neglect*, 21, 391-398.

Hatcher, R., Trussell, J., Stewart, F., Stewart, G., Kowal, D., Guest, F., Cates, W., & Policar, M. (1994). *Contraceptive Technology* (16th ed.). New York: Irvington.

Ivey, J. (1997). The adolescent with pelvic inflammatory disease: Assessment and management. *The Nurse Practitioner*, February, 78-91.

Laumann, E., Gagnon, J., Michael, R., & Michaels, S. (1994). *The Social Organization of Sexuality: Sexual Practices in the United States*. Chicago: University of Chicago Press.

Moran, G. (1997). Diagnosing STDs, *Emergency Medicine*, January/February.

Orr, D., Langefeld, C., Katz, B., Caine, V., Dias, P., Blythe, M., & Jones, R. (1992). Factors associated with condom use among sexually active female adolescents. *Journal of Pediatrics*, 120, 311-317.

Pleck, J., Sonenstein, F., & Ku, L. (1993). Changes in adolescent males' use of and attitudes toward condoms, 1988-1991. *Family Planning Perspectives*, 25, 106-109 & 117.

Polit-O'Hara, D., & Kahn, J. (1985). Communication and adolescent contraceptive practices in adolescent couples. *Adolescence*, 20, 33-43.

Poppen, P. (1994). Adolescent contraceptive use and communication: Changes over a decade. *Adolescence*, 29, 503-514.

Post, S., & Botkin, J. (1995). Adolescents and HIV prevention. *Clinical Pediatrics*, 34, 41-45.

Seidman, S., & Rieder, R. (1994). A review of sexual behavior in the United States. *American Journal of Psychiatry, 151,* 330-341.

Shafer, M. (1997). Lower abdominal pain and the adolescent girl. *Emergency Medicine,* February, 91-99.